PRESIDENT

LIGHTBOX
openlightbox.com

Sara Cucini

LIGHTBOX

Go to
www.openlightbox.com
and enter this book's
unique code.

ACCESS CODE

LBXT6386

Lightbox is an all-inclusive digital solution for the teaching and learning of curriculum topics in an original, groundbreaking way. Lightbox is based on National Curriculum Standards.

OPTIMIZED FOR

- ✓ TABLETS
- ✓ SMART BOARDS
- ✓ COMPUTERS
- ✓ AND MUCH MORE!

STANDARD FEATURES OF LIGHTBOX

- **AUDIO** High-quality narration using text-to-speech system
- **VIDEOS** Embedded high-definition video clips
- **ACTIVITIES** Printable PDFs that can be emailed and graded
- **WEBLINKS** Curated links to external, child-safe resources
- **SLIDESHOWS** Pictorial overviews of key concepts
- **INTERACTIVE MAPS** Interactive maps and aerial satellite imagery
- **QUIZZES** Ten multiple choice questions that are automatically graded and emailed for teacher assessment
- **KEY WORDS** Matching key concepts to their definitions

SUPPLEMENTARY RESOURCES

- **SHARE** Share titles within your Learning Management System (LMS) or Library Circulation System
- **CURRICULUM** Find national and state curriculum correlations
- **CITATION** Create bibliographical references following APA, CMSO, and MLA styles

VIDEOS

WEBLINKS

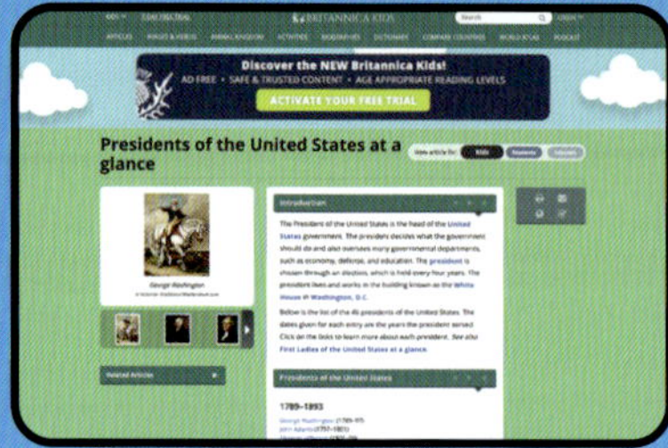

SLIDESHOWS

QUIZZES

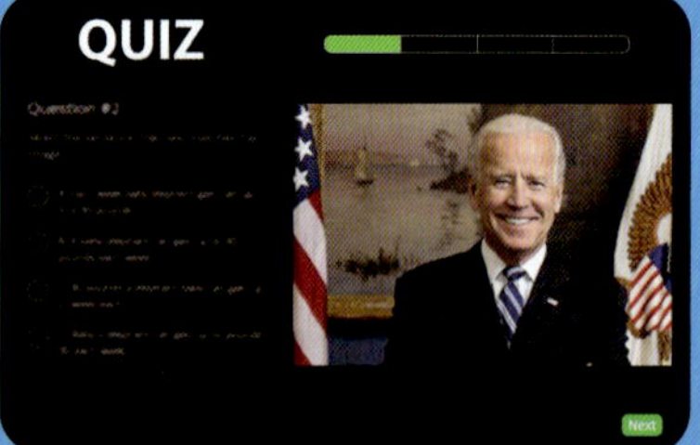

This title is part of our Lightbox digital subscription

2

1-Year K–2 Subscription
ISBN 978-1-5105-5423-8

Access hundreds of Lightbox titles with our digital subscription.
Sign up for a **FREE** subscription trial at **www.openlightbox.com/trial**

The digital components of this book are guaranteed to stay active for at least five years from the date of publication.

PRESIDENT

Contents

Our Government

The U.S. federal government has three different branches that work together.

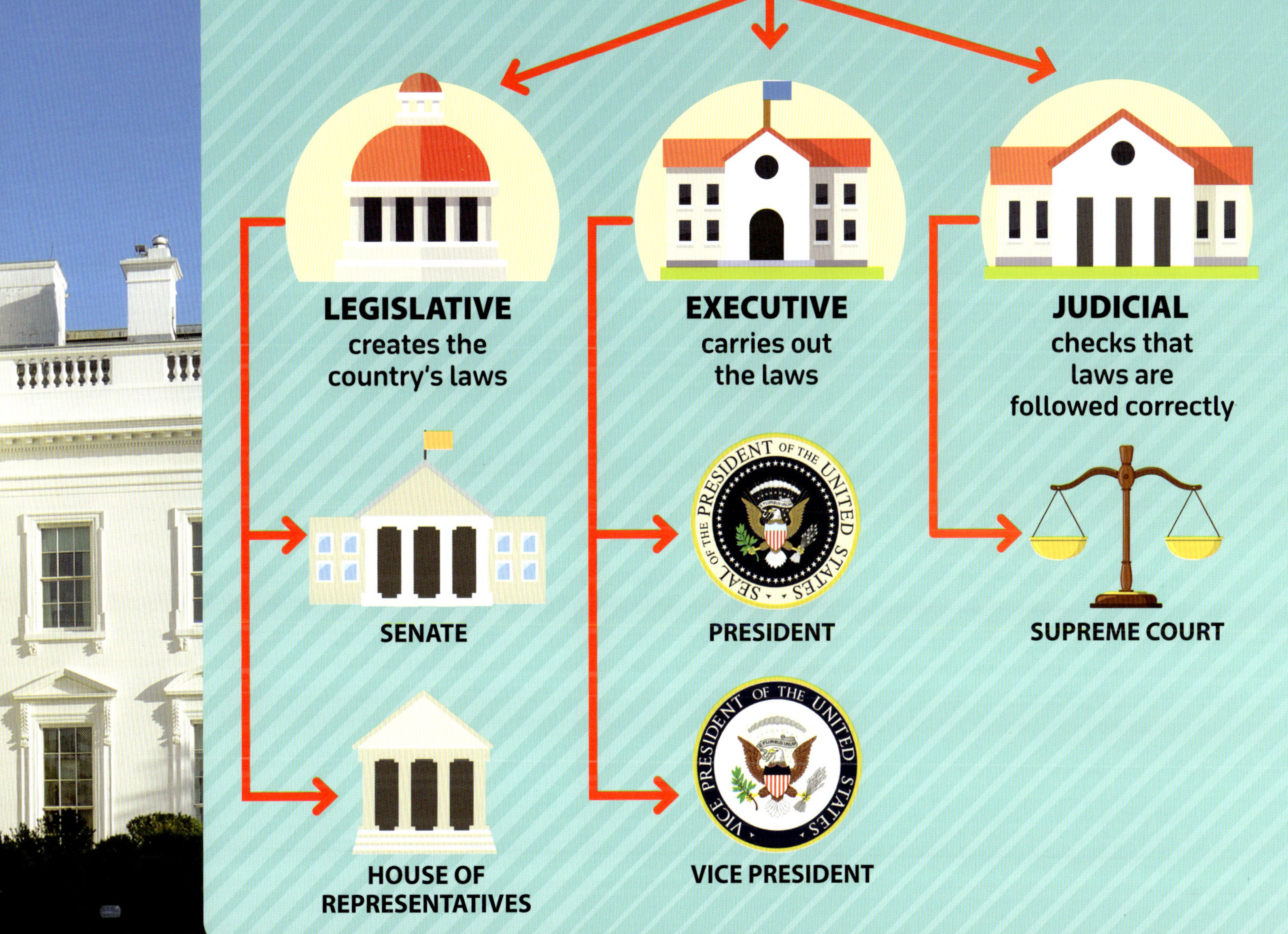
Branches of the Federal Government
LEGISLATIVE
creates the country's laws
EXECUTIVE
carries out the laws
JUDICIAL
checks that laws are followed correctly
SENATE
PRESIDENT
SUPREME COURT
HOUSE OF REPRESENTATIVES
VICE PRESIDENT

Who Is the President?

The president of the United States leads the executive branch. It is the president's responsibility to make sure that the country's laws are applied. He or she also controls the work of everyone else who belongs to the executive branch.

ESIDENT OF THE UNITED

What Does the President Do?

The president represents the people of the United States. He or she is the head of the U.S. government. The president is also the commander-in-chief of the U.S. armed forces.

Presidential History

George Washington was the first U.S. president. He became president in 1789. The United States has had 44 other people serve as president since George Washington.

Presidential Records

First Woman to Run for President

Victoria Claflin Woodhull ran in the 1872 presidential elections.

Youngest President

Theodore Roosevelt was 42 when he became president, in 1901.

Oldest President

Joe Biden was 78 when he began his presidency, in 2021.

Who Can Be President?

Not everyone can be president. To become president, a person must meet three requirements.

1 Be an American citizen born in the United States

2 Be at least 35 years old

3 Have lived in the country for at least 14 years in a row

Becoming President

Presidents are elected every four years. The presidential election is always held on the first Tuesday of November. People across the United States vote to decide who will become president.

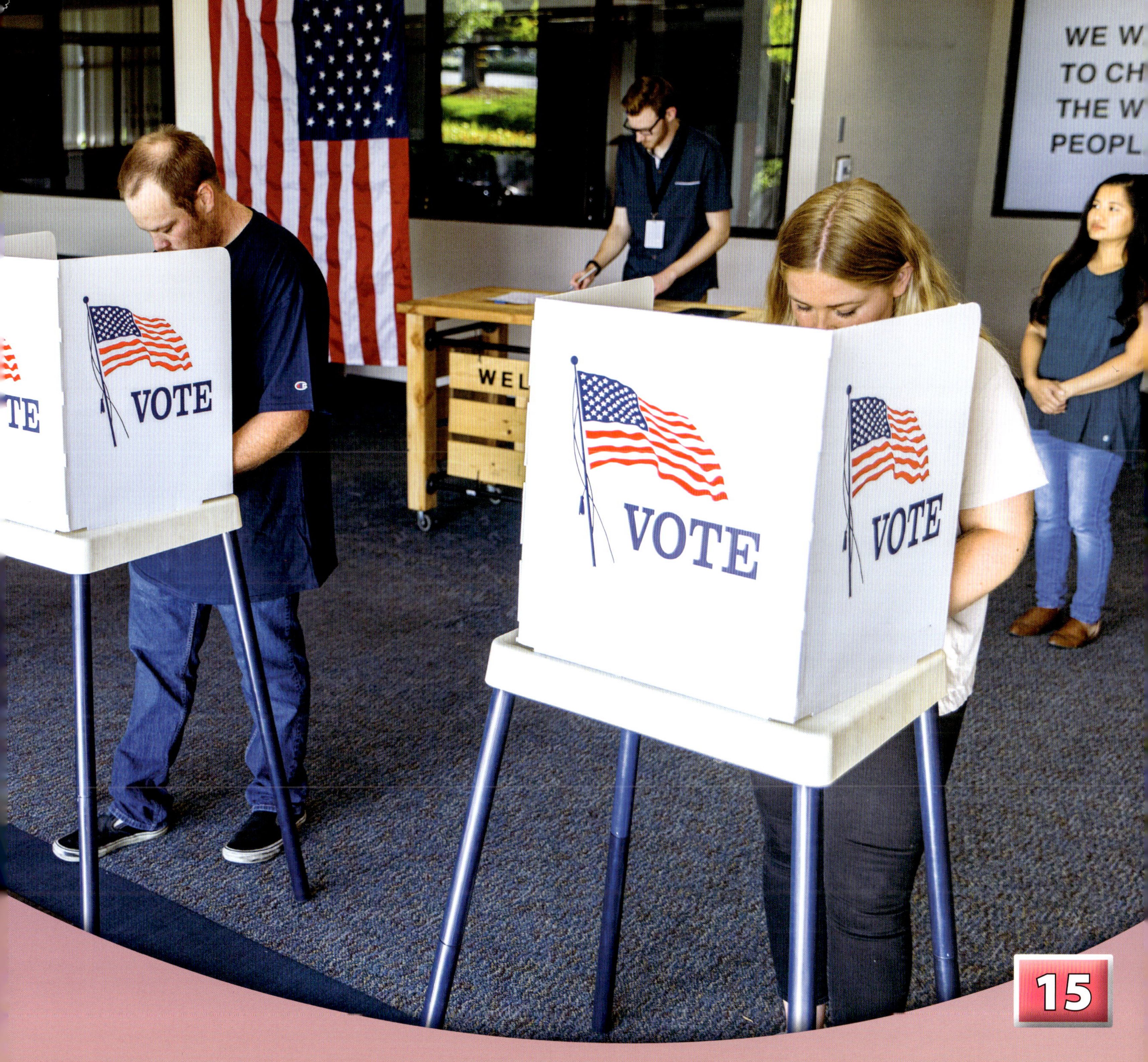
VOTE
VOTE
VOTE

The White House

The president lives and works in a building called the White House.

1792 The year **construction** began on the White House

1600 Pennsylvania Avenue NW
The **address** of the White House in Washington, DC

1800 The year **John Adams**, the first president to live in the White House, moved into the building

Signing the Laws

The president can sign the bills passed by the House of Representatives and the Senate into law. The president can also reject a bill if he or she thinks that it is not the best choice for the country. This is called the power of veto.

SEAL OF THE PRESIDENT OF THE UNITED STATES

Traveling the World

The president represents the United States abroad. He or she often travels to meet with leaders of other countries. The president works together with these leaders to solve problems that affect the entire world.

AIR FORCE ONE

2 Airplanes available for the president

4,000 SQUARE FEET

The total space available for the president on each Air Force One airplane (370 square meters)

AT LEAST 8,000 MILES

The distance each Air Force One airplane can fly before refueling (12,900 kilometers)

What Have You Learned?

The president is the head of the executive branch.

The president represents the people of the United States.

The president is the commander-in-chief.

The president signs bills into law.

The president represents the United States abroad.

VOTE
VOTE
VOTE
VOTE
SEAL OF THE PRESIDENT OF THE UNITED STATES

KEY WORDS

Research has shown that as much as 65 percent of all written material published in English is made up of 300 words. These 300 words cannot be taught using pictures or learned by sounding them out. They must be recognized by sight. This book contains 73 common sight words to help young readers improve their reading fluency and comprehension. This book also teaches young readers several important content words, such as proper nouns. These words are paired with pictures to aid in learning and improve understanding.

Page	Sight Words First Appearance
4	different, has, our, that, the, three, together, work
5	are, country, house, of, out
6	also, every, he, it, make, or, she, states, to, who
9	do, does, head, in, is, people, what
10	as, first, had, other, was
11	began, for, his, run, when
13	a, American, an, at, be, can, have, must, not, old, years
14	always, four, on, will
17	and, into, lives, white
18	by, if, this, thinks
20	often, these, with, world
21	air, before, each, feet, miles, one

Page	Content Words First Appearance
4	branches, government
5	House of Representatives, laws, president, Senate, Supreme Court, vice president
6	responsibility, United States
9	armed forces, commander-in-chief, leader
10	George Washington, history
11	elections, Joe Biden, presidency, records, Theodore Roosevelt, Victoria Claflin Woodhull, woman
13	citizen, requirements, row
14	November, Tuesday
17	address, building, construction, John Adams, Washington, DC, White House
18	bills, choice, power of veto
20	problems
21	Air Force One, airplanes, distance, space

Published by Lightbox Learning Inc.
276 5th Avenue, Suite 704 #917
New York, NY 10001
Website: www.openlightbox.com

Library of Congress Control Number: 2023949280

ISBN 978-1-5105-6759-7 (hardcover)
ISBN 978-1-5105-8103-6 (multi-user eBook)

Printed in Guangzhou, China
1 2 3 4 5 6 7 8 9 0 27 26 25 24 23

112023
110822

Project Coordinator: Sara Cucini
Designer: Jean Faye Marie Rodriguez

Every reasonable effort has been made to trace ownership and to obtain permission to reprint copyright material. The publisher would be pleased to have any errors or omissions brought to its attention so that they may be corrected in subsequent printings.

The publisher acknowledges Alamy, Getty Images, Shutterstock, and Wikimedia Commons as the primary image suppliers for this title.